AFTER THE POINT OF NO RETURN

DAVID WAGONER

After the Point
of No Return

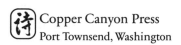 Copper Canyon Press
Port Townsend, Washington

Copper Canyon Press is in residence at Fort Worden State Park in Port Townsend, Washington, under the auspices of Centrum. Centrum is a gathering place for artists and creative thinkers from around the world, students of all ages and backgrounds, and audiences seeking extraordinary cultural enrichment.

LIBRARY OF CONGRESS CATALOGING-IN-PUBLICATION DATA

Wagoner, David.
After the point of no return / David Wagoner.
   p.   cm.
ISBN 978-1-55659-382-6 (pbk.)
1. Title.
PS3545.A345A69 2012
811'.54—dc23

                                                                2011043021

9 8 7 6 5 4 3 2 FIRST PRINTING

COPPER CANYON PRESS
Post Office Box 271
Port Townsend, Washington 98368

www.coppercanyonpress.org

These are all for Robin with love.

ACKNOWLEDGMENTS

Thanks to the editors of the following publications, in which these poems first appeared: *AGNI:* "Striking the Set"; *American Literary Review:* "Falling into Place," "Our Bodies," "In the Nursing Home"; *Antioch Review:* "Meeting a Stranger"; *Asheville Poetry Review:* "Orpheus Practicing"; *Bellevue Literary Review:* "A Brief History," "In a Greenhouse," "For Their Second Childhood," "The Name"; *The Chariton Review:* "Playground"; *Christianity and Literature:* "In the Congregational Basement"; *The Cimarron Review:* "Onstage"; *The Cincinnati Review:* "Running the Four Hundred Meters," "Life Class"; *The Connecticut Poetry Review:* "Rain Dance in a Rain Forest," "Overheard at Dinner in the Home of a Recent Widow"; *Crazyhorse:* "The Cherry Tree"; *Ecotone:* "A Footnote to the History of the New York Central Railroad," "Thoreau and the Loose Cow," "Thoreau and the Lightning," "A Preface to the History of Chairs"; *Free Lunch:* "A Beginner's Guide to Death"; *Field:* "Mother's Night"; *Five Points:* "Among Brambles," "The Minutes of the Last Meeting"; *The Georgia Review:* "Rooming with Jesus"; *The Gettysburg Review:* "The Last Good Hour of a Worker Bee," "Under Fire"; *Hampden-Sydney Poetry Review:* "The Fun House," "The Hazards of Serenading," "The General Theory"; *Hanging Loose:* "At the Farewell Performance of Henry Ellsworth Robinson, the Magician Known as Ching Ling Soo," "At the Ostrich Farm," "The Salute"; *The Hudson Review:* "That Night in London," "A Zodiac for the Twenty-Second Century," "A Cold Call"; *Indiana Review:* "The Ends of My Fingers"; *The Iowa Review:* "By a Creek," "By the Empty Stone"; *Margie:* "Pleasant Dreams," "Panic"; *The Minnesota Review:* "Kissing Cousins"; *New Letters:* "A Letter to an Old Poet"; *New Ohio Review:* "Walking Along the Beach with a Five-Year-Old," "The Boy Who Ran Away from Me," "Breakfast with Salesmen before the Poetry Reading"; *North American Review:* "Preaching to the Choir"; *Ocho:* "Foxhole," "Coolness under Fire"; *On Earth:* "By a Pond"; *The Paris Review:* "Photographing Snakes"; *Pleiades:* "Signing," "This Is Only a Test," "Pounding Swords into Ploughshares"; *Poetry:* "Going Back to the Sea"; *Poetry Miscellany:* "Being a Model"; *Potomac Review:* "Aristotle Comes to a Conclusion," "Your Tree," "What the Marine Biologist Told Me"; *Prairie Schooner:* "Driving," "Dust Devil," "Lost in Thought on an Extension Ladder," "Off Balance"; *Rattle:* "Before the Poetry Reading," "In Memory of His Memory"; *Redactions:* "Pig Dance"; *River Styx:* "The Fly," "Instructions for the Caretaker"; *Salmagundi:* "Writing for Money"; *Shenandoah:* "Convivium," "Marksmanship"; *Southern Poetry Review:* "For My Daughters during Their First Penumbral Eclipse"; *Sou'wester:* "On the Persistence of Metaphor"; *The Threepenny Review:* "The Bitter End"; *Tri-Quarterly:* "Ashes," "At Dawn on the Fifth of July"; *Western Humanities Review:* "My Father's Body," "My Lost Uncles," "How to Live," "Never Let Your Characters Sit Down," "On the Road," "Helping the Home Patient Fall Asleep"; *The Yale Review:* "On Being Asked Once More What a Poem Is," "Long Overdue Praise for Her," "Listening."

Contents

3

4

5

I

After the Point of No Return

After that moment when you've lost all reason
for going back where you started, when going ahead
is no longer a yes or no but a matter of fact,
you'll need to weigh, on the one hand, what will seem
on the other, almost nothing against something
slightly more than nothing and must choose
again and again, at points of fewer and fewer
chances to guess, when and which way to turn.

That's when you might stop thinking about stars
and storm clouds, the direction of wind,
the difference between rain and snow, the time
of day or the lay of the land, about which trees
mean water, which birds know what you need
to know before it's too late, or what's right here
under your feet, no longer able to tell you
where it was you thought you had to go.

A Brief History

A poet writes the history of his body.
HENRY DAVID THOREAU, THE JOURNAL

Where it went, what it came back to,
where and why it laid itself down
and tried to sleep, what happened to it
without advice or consent,
what it failed at, how it disobeyed
its own commands to no purpose,
what it held in its hands when it was told
and told to let go, what it neglected
to open its arms for, how it wouldn't
stand still, not even when it might as well
have had no legs at all
to be running away with, or the times
when it would sit and wait
without knowing what it was waiting for
in places where it didn't belong,
how it broke down, how
but not why it made marks again
and again on pieces of paper.

The Ends of My Fingers

I was listening to the man
on the radio plucking strings
with his fingers and fingernails
and telling us how to play.

I was holding the open doors
of our upright cabinet
and feeling so full of music
I lifted my whole body,

and the radio toppled toward me
and slammed me to the floor.
The edge cut off the ends
of two of my right fingers.

My mother, who could sing
and play on the piano,
carried me in her arms
through the bleeding living room,

through the front door and down
the steps while we both sang
a song I'd never heard,
across our yard to the house

where the old doctor lived,
where I sat in his lap, where my mother
gave him the two red ends,
and then we went on singing

while he clamped them on again
and wrapped them out of sight.
He told me not to look
inside or try to find out

what color they might be.
He said *he'd* open them
like a present with *his* fingers
next week when I was three.

The Fun House

You're supposed to go inside. They're showing you
how to get up the steps and through the door
into a narrow hallway where it's dark,
where someone's laughing over a loudspeaker.

Whoever's holding your hand lets go of it.
You put one shoe ahead of another shoe
to show you remember how. What looks like a window
has a doorknob on it that turns and turns and turns

when you turn it, but doesn't work. You see somebody
scary in front of you. You both open
your mouths at the same time, and it's you
in a mirror. The floor goes crooked. It's jiggling.

You have to go but there's nowhere to go.
Too many lights go on, and suddenly
go back off before you can shut your eyes.
Somebody ugly's under a white sheet.

You're being sick on a rug that cost good money.

Convivium

In memoriam Emily Carlson

After we'd redivided
Gaul into twenty-three parts,
our seventh-grade Latin class
in sandals and off-white togas
threw a *convivium*.

Over the fried chicken
our *haruspex* announced the signs
as *bene, bene, bene,*
so we pitched and proved
we could conjugate, decline,
and define some verbs and nouns
sometimes almost as well
as Miss Emily Carlson.

All fall she'd listened to us
mumble and mispronounce
with a set smile on her face
and at least one eye half closed
behind thick horn-rim glasses.
We failed her, and she passed us.

She believed we were carrying on
some semiclassical
tradition, if not for her sake,
for our own, that at least a few
of the *radices* she'd watered
in our poor soil wouldn't shrivel
but would finally rise and shine.

When all our games were over
and after she'd handed out
the small *edulis* prizes,
wrapped and trimmed and inscribed
with her own neat, careful *digits,*
she shouted toward the ceiling
an *exclamatio*
and fell down on the floor
and began to shake, shudder,
and jitter the whole length
of her gray dress, her mouth
uttering through white foam
untranslatable words,
then died *post meridiem.*
Oh sunt lacrimae rerum.

Driving

You were behind the wheel
of the used family car
>   at night with no license,
>   no key. It turned on
all by itself. You could see
through the dusty windshield,
>   not the garage wall
>   but the road ahead
running under. It was yours.
It wasn't yours. You knew
>   where both your feet should go
>   and when to lift them and why,
what never, never to change
till exactly the right time
>   as you picked up speed,
>   but not where you were going,
except when you had to shut
the driver's door behind you,
>   tiptoe up the stairs
>   and climb back into bed.

In the Congregational Basement

On an old piece of plywood
the size of a Ping-Pong table
we built Jerusalem
out of oatmeal, flour, and water.

When Reverend MacLaurie showed us
pictures, we knuckled down
and did it with bare hands,
all thirty of which, if left
idle a little too long,
might have done the devil's work
instead of the carpenter's.

We bulldozed crooked streets
with thumbs and Popsicle sticks,
made temples and huts and Christ
knew what out of cardboard.

We painted it brown and gold,
poured dunes out of real sand,
and stuck real rocks on hills
and out-of-proportion horses
and chariots, not on fire,
but on roads, and then we played
Bible games for an hour,
and Jerusalem wasn't looking
too good when we went home.

And the next Sunday, after
Reverend MacLaurie sang

a song by William Blake,
we had to scrape Jerusalem off
into cans out in the alley.

Kissing Cousins

In Grandma's kitchen garden, while whip-poor-wills
whooped softly between the lettuce and red beets,
my lips as dry as hers, my left hand trembling
in hers like hers, my right arm reaching almost
halfway around her through that breathless evening,
not knowing how to, I kissed Ada Rose.

She was as wide as Grandma, but for miles
there was no one else I could kiss, and the girls back home
played spin the bottle with older boys, not me,
and I'd been dreaming of girls with their clothes off,
and here stood Cousin Ada Rose in a garden.

We didn't breathe because I didn't dare
so close to her glasses and because she couldn't
with her mouth shut tight against the deepest longings
of asthma. With a gasp and a glancing blow
of the hips we parted, and I sneaked upstairs
to hide my life under a comforter.

If only I'd kissed her hard with a hard grin
like Humphrey Bogart, cracking some kind of joke,
or given her a sister's birthday peck
or a Jimmy Cagney smack smack on the cheek.
But I'd done it scared and solemn, a dumb cowboy
forgetting when to head into the sunset.

All night, sleeping and waking, I tried to do it
differently while the curtains billowed toward me
like nightgowns, like the vapor from the machine

that breathed in her bedroom. In the glare of morning
I sat cold on a bus, my vacation over,
while Ada Rose, tight-lipped, didn't wave goodbye.

A Footnote to the History of the
New York Central Railroad

Grand Central bustled at one end of it
and Chicago's Union Station roared at the other,
all its miles the result of chairmen of boards
and barons and superintendents and stockholders
determined to keep the original colonies
connected to the heartland, and down the graded
slope to division managers, to subordinate
section managers and section bosses
and their section gangs responsible for the tracks,
for keeping them straight and steady and well tamped
with gravel around and under the crossties
weatherproofed with creosote. There the tie plates,
held in place by spikes, gripped at the rails
and held them down for miles and miles and miles
while freight and passengers rumbled over them.

A fifteen-year-old boy with an imaginary
Social Security card and loud instructions
and daily demonstrations, for two long weeks
for a few long yards in a switchyard west of Gary,
with a spike maul, whose head was exactly the same
size as the head of the spike, kept trying to hit one
square on the head and didn't and couldn't and quit.

My Father's Body

It was always ready to get up in the evening
or afternoon or morning—that depended
on whatever week it was—and he could put
clothes on it and understand which holes
were for legs and which were for arms, and how some nights
the already-knotted necktie had to be squeezed
under a collar and clinched under its chin.

It was the force around wrenches, behind saws,
the pivot of sledgehammers and ax blades,
and though he couldn't teach it to float in water,
he could make it stand its ground under red showers
of molten steel and shrug them off without flinching.
He knew which kind of easy chair it would fit
and, as it fell asleep there, how to keep it
sitting up till he could take it to bed.

My Lost Uncles

In memory of Otterbein Siffert and Campbell Banyard

They couldn't talk right. They couldn't trust their mouths
to say what they meant to say or meant to mean.
One couldn't smile without remembering
he had too little to smile with. The other heard
always the hollowness of what was missing
above his tongue, so kept his voice to himself.

They both turned shy. When they came up against
too many mirrors, too many listeners
too close to home, both of them disappeared,
one out on the prairie north of the Badlands,
the other somewhere south along the Ohio.
They never came back to say anything else.

Lost uncles, I have a smaller kind of trouble
making these words about you. The effort seems
awkward and clumsy here on a piece of paper.
You kept more quiet than others. You listened longer
and seemed to have less to offer, but you had more
than you ever had a chance to say out loud.

I hope you both found places where words were easy
to let out of your mouths, where someone heard
everything you said without being sorry.
One of you heard the wind and one heard water.
You followed them out of sight. Though both of you
are still far out of sight, I'm listening.

Mother's Night

She's celebrating it for me. She's coming back
from the place where she was scattered, from the place
where she was introduced to medical students
and their teachers and was slowly taken apart,
back from where she lost herself among nurses,
from what was left of her house, from her single bed,
from her sink and her kitchen window where she could see
the dead stalks in her garden. She's coming back,
her arms full of the flowers I gave her once
a year in April, and she's asking me
to put them back on the stems in the greenhouses
they came from, to let them shrink away from the light.

Onstage

I took a director to a waterfall
with an actress, his younger mistress,
to show how wild the world could be
offstage. All day and all night
the creek for centuries had been rushing
through a narrow, shaded passage
over a sheer drop. We stood near the edge
where a cedar had toppled from one side
to the other like a bad bridge. Without a word
he led her down to the mossy, half-rotten trunk
and began walking across.

I'd dreamed of being afraid to do it,
but wouldn't have dreamed
of doing it. I might have crawled partway
with my eyes shut, under a gun,
but there they were, crossing in street shoes.

Her stage and backstage lives
were already in his hands. She had already
been putting her only body
where he'd told her to,
had changed her face dozens of times to please him,
had tried to remake (part by part)
herself into all the women he'd wanted her to be,
and she hadn't been good enough at it.
The cast and crew predicted she'd disappear
at the end of the season.

I watched them walking, shakily, afraid
my minor part would be to climb down there
to their dead bodies in a pool.
It wasn't something I wanted to break a leg for.

I'm leaving them midstream in this melodrama
to tell you the subplot: the woman beside me
(wearing my ring) through all her early years
had majored in wanting to go to Hollywood,
had bleached her hair and gone, had slept around
for a while, had cut her wrists
very carefully three times, had given up,
and had threatened to jump from bridges higher than this one.

She was looking at this couple
and following their careers
with an uneasy, bitter amusement—
another actress losing herself in her role.

We had been lovers once
by this falling water, which was still performing
what it was meant to perform,
with an endless roar containing
and concealing all the vowels of human speech.

We were speechless.
We didn't know what to do
with our hands or feet. We had no more
to say to ourselves or to the other pair
(who had made it across and were acting proud),
and we didn't know what to say on the way home.

Walking Along the Beach with a Five-Year-Old

She thinks she has a pretty good idea
what seaweed is. *It's bushes under water.*
And half a clamshell doesn't call for words

from either of us, so we send it sailing
back to the shallows to fulfill itself.
When asked, I try to explain what a heap of kelp

is doing above the tide line, bladders and holdfasts
shrinking from so much air, but I stop
short when sand fleas jump out of the folds.

I redirect her attention to the horizon,
where the setting sun is doing something more
familiar to her, but she goes wading ahead

to concentrate on the carcass of a scoter
still trailing the black feathers of one wing.
She stoops to pick it up (one thumb, one finger

as precise as a gull's beak) and holds it dripping
halfway out of the arriving surf
and looks up at me sideways. Our eyes meet.

She seems to be accusing me of something
she can't yet say out loud. I hear
my teacher's impassioned voice recite John Donne:

I have a sin of fear, that when I have spun
My last thread, I shall perish on the shore,
but keep it to myself. She lets the bird fall

back to where it had been and balances
her brand-new body above the water and sand
and against the wind splashes ahead of me.

Pleasant Dreams

She's seven. She's afraid
            to go to sleep tonight
                    because when she lies down
the bad thoughts come rushing into her head,
            come rushing over her quilt, the bears
                    and horses and elephants and bad rabbits,
and jump into her dreams. I tell her
            it's all right, everything's going to be
                    all right, nothing can harm you, sleep
is your best friend, we love you, there's nothing
            ever to be afraid of, and now, now there,
                    there, think of the night-light
all the way till breakfast, and look
            what I'm going to do. I'm tiptoeing
                    into another room and lying down
while the mattress and the floor melt under me
            and the walls fly up and I hear the call of the green
                    dental assistant as the laughing gas
wears off and the whole idea of morning
            is torn out by the roots and goes *clink*
                    in a basin and the drowned man
in his translucent body bag
            worms his way out of the morgue
                    and slips on his form-fitting cassock
trimmed with gauze and chases the interns
            out of the swinging doors into the garden
                    where visitors have left baskets and baskets
of vegetables to rot into compost
            among the artificial flowers in memory
                    of the dear, dear, nearly deadly departed.

For My Daughters during Their First Penumbral Eclipse

Although I'm telling them once more the sun
is larger than the Earth and the moon smaller,
that large sources of light cast two-toned shadows
beyond small objects, they refuse to remember.

I've joined those other teachers trying to show them
everything that's known about erring stars,
who've graded them slightly down for believing in something
else out of their dream-filled love for the sky.

If they won't puzzle out the solar system,
why should I scold them? Neither would Sherlock Holmes
or the wisest wise men before Copernicus.
They all settled for nests of crystal spheres.

Emerson said a kind of light shines through us
and makes us aware we're nothing. "Nothing" seems wrong.
We transmit something or other. We interfere.
Cosmically speaking, we have a nuisance value.

And nobody knows why, not even today,
not even the first that rounded the sun-kissed moon,
tongue-tied with wonder, garbling old testaments,
just barely raising moondust while sleepwalking.

Though the Earth has caught our moon in the outer cone
of its double shadow for a while this evening,
at dawn the sun will make up for lost time
by spinning fire around all daughters of men.

Playground

My daughters are both playing
under the sun this morning,
in and out of the shade
on primary-colored swings
and slides and spiral ladders,
and they're being just as good
as can be at tagging others.

They're among the most evasive
(when they're not It) and clever
enough (when they are)
to touch the ones they're after.
I'm proud watching over them
from my safe place on the bench.

A man sits next to me.
His long gray hair hangs down
the back of his wrinkled coat.
He's wearing a yachting cap,
thick glasses, a woman's skirt,
sneakers with open toes,
and blue-and-white batting gloves.

He's holding much of his life
ready to eat or wear
in a plastic shopping bag.
He leans my way and offers
the part of it that's french fries
and tells me I'd better help
myself or be sorry later.

And now two women are guiding
three disadvantaged children
out of a van. A girl,
maybe eleven, who scuttles
to a sandbox and sits down,
laughing. A younger boy
who knows how to run and clamber
up onto a platform
and straddle a tunnel slide.
A teenage Latina, her arms
akimbo, who smiles around
at the wide world of sports.
All three are as pale as if trained
to grow up in the dark.

The girl in the sand is squealing,
lifting, and letting fly
whatever these handfuls are.
The boy up in the air,
eyes shut in ecstasy,
is pounding his blue drum.
The Latina is strutting around
on the grass like a mistress
of ceremonies, waving
as if to coax applause
or to congratulate
herself for winning something
by shaking most of the hands
of most of the babysitters

within reach, including mine
and the two in batting gloves
beside me, that go on shaking
hers over and over
and won't let go till she sees
he's as proud of her as a father.

The Boy Who Ran Away from Me

He was in a tree, up there in what I thought
    was my own orchard, putting overripe apples
        inside his shirt, and I hurried out of the house
to tell him for godsake to be careful,
    and the first words out of my mouth were
        All right, all right, it's all right,
don't hurt yourself, but he must have heard
    some grown-up yelling, *Get the hell out of there,*
        and he fell down in a zigzag,
grabbing and half catching
    at air, at branches even heavier
        with apples then he was, ten feet
to an earth already covered with soggy windfall
    that cold October morning. He ran away
        limping, a ten-year-old crying
for what I was probably going to tell his father,
    but didn't. And here I am, still standing
        under that tree, watching him trying to scramble
over a picket fence without losing
    everything way back then, still telling him
        to come back soon, to have some more,
to bring his brother and somebody's sister next time
    to help me pick them before it was too late,
        before I'd be wakened again and again in the night
by the least touch of wind or rain
    and wonder how he was and hear
        the rest of them falling and lying there in the grass.

2

A Letter to an Old Poet

Do you believe you are a poet? If so, then what you must do
is obvious.

RAINER MARIA RILKE, *LETTERS TO A YOUNG POET*

Do you still believe, old man, you are a poet?
If so, what you must do is so obvious,
you shouldn't need reminding. You should keep trying
to do whatever you haven't done or start
doing again what you didn't manage to do
right in the first place. You should stay alive
as often as possible and keep yourself open
to anything out of place and everything
with nowhere else to go, to carry what's left
of your voice out and beyond, into, over,
and under, past, within, outside, between,
among, across, along, and up and around
and to be beside yourself when the spirit moves you
and to thank Miss Clippinger for your prepositions.

How to Live

Poets show us how to live.
MATTHEW ARNOLD

They show us more often
than not how to die
at the same time and in more ways
   of doing both, of taking the first
   out of the heart of the other
   and spreading it around
and making it up, making it over
in legendary examples
in the sand after falling
   into the bad company
   of themselves, too early
   and too late, and too soon
they forget how to live
through it and still be able
to follow in strange tracks
   on paper. Their embarrassing lives
   make schoolteachers labor
   hard to explain why
they dared to take so much
that was harmful into their mouths
and swallow it, to neglect
   (not trying to recollect)
   their debts to others, to forget
   to do what they were meant to
before giving away
or ignoring their last chances
with a half-conscious flourish

with one hand waving or still holding
someone's hand while the other
keeps scribbling something
or other, keeps on trying
with the equivalent of a feather
to put everything down.

Writing for Money

No man but a blockhead ever wrote except for money.
DR. SAMUEL JOHNSON

In seventh grade, I had my first two shots
at writing for money. The American Legion's
essay contest asked me to spread myself
on The Meaning of the American Flag, so I did.

In lines as long as the family typewriter
could make on a page, I told them what it meant.
I wrote star-spangled bursts of Betsy Ross
redder, whiter, and bluer than anyone else.

They paid me twenty dollars to read it out loud
on the sidewalk outside the Whiting (Indiana)
police garage. When I was through, old men
in blue and khaki uniforms beat their drums.

The Indiana Anti-Saloon League
(not quite as grand as Women's Christian Temperance)
challenged us students, all the way from South Bend
to Terra Haute, from Roby to Evansville,

to write about The Effects of Alcohol
on the Human Body. I quoted the best facts
from a pamphlet somebody left behind in church
and, sober as my judges, made up the rest.

I won. They sent me a check for fifteen dollars.
I've written lots more since. For most of it
Dr. Johnson would call me an old blockhead,
and he'd be right. Here's one more page of proof.

That Night in London

That night in London Stephen Spender said
come to my party Allen Tate is passing
through again on his way somewhere we went
in our Guggenheim suit and tie to St. John's Wood
to stand foursquare beside Sir Herbert Read
the multilateral critic of everything
in his narrow worsted disinclined-to-argue-
with gin-and-it for the purpose of agreement
under a widespread hat like the small roof
of a gazebo Rose Macaulay the center pole
sustaining the Near East for likes of Cyril
Connelly's vested interest in hors d'oeuvres
between John Hayward's thumb and middle finger
out from under the Thomist tom-tom sternum
of Eliotic outsiders beside his wheelchair
where Colin Wilson was heeling and pointing out
with flushed-to-the-eyeballs tweedy Henry Reed
naming his parts indifferently for the amusement
of oracular almost-sober Louis MacNeice
whose bagpipe gaze caught Sonia Orwell ready
to leave the guest of honor having delivered
to his own event one macrocephalic Tate
hard by her elbow cocked for the remainder
and loaded now for the immediate future
but not for hers we asked ourselves in the doorway
have we risen to this occasion or talked our way
out of it for good god who can remember
anything anyone said to anybody
at a literary blur with all our eyes

off center out of focus meanwhile Stephen
was saying please drop by tomorrow evening
to benefit the Hungarian Revolution.

The Hazards of Serenading

Romeo, Don Giovanni, Cyrano,
and Percy Shelley, to name only a few,
poured out their passions under balconies,
sincerely, cynically, professionally,
or breathlessly and wound up poisoned, in hell,
skewered, or out cold. And Juliet,
Elvira, Roxanne, and the musky maid of Kashmir
either died young or married somebody else.

Preaching to the Choir

Worshippers who can sing
(or try to) don't want their faith
taken for granted. They long for
melodic turns of phrase
and memorable cadences.
They'd be listening in the pews
if they hadn't needed to make
music of empty air.

Any tone-deaf preacher
had better do his damnedest
as an off-the-beat, white-throaty,
black-robed, timorous,
sharp, flat soloist
for critically minded singers
sitting there behind him,
flinching at his droning
and trying to forgive him
for conducting only himself
and turning his back on them.

Breakfast with Salesmen before the Poetry Reading

They sell themselves to each other
over eggs over easy and tell each other the tale,
give the high sign and the low five,
and nudge their servers to show they understand
their touching problems. They know, they know
where they're coming from, but just kidding around
to pass the time before they're back on the road
again, so good at being sincere,
they don't even have to try. I feel left out
at first, unable to share anything
but pepper and salt, but now I'm heading down
the same steps and the same rough road with them
to make my pitch, my own prepared, polite
cold calls this morning, to give my usual spiel
out loud to some tough customers, to give
easy answers to harder and harder questions.

On Being Asked Once More What a Poem Is

Instead of another song and dance from the book —
Memorable speech or *Statements made*
on the way to the grave or *Whatever*
(*when I think of it*) *makes me cut myself*
shaving or *The spontaneous overflow*
of powerful feelings recollected and so on —
this time, this time not a set speech or a painful
minimumbly muttered evasion
with a dying fall or a cutting edge. Let's try
a more romantic movement, the song and dance
themselves, almost in person, for this young man
sprawled in the front row, a hip-hop logo
glued to his notebook. *Why do you listen to songs?*
What is a song? Why don't you sing one for us?
If you can't sing, recite the words of one.
If you can't remember the words, make up your own.
If they don't sound right without music,
make up some music. If you don't know how,
then play somebody else's. If you can't play,
then dance. Are you a dancer? Has anyone seen you
dancing lately? Why were you doing it?
Were you listening to singers while you were dancing?
Were they singing words? Were you humming
some of those words to yourself or to a partner
opposite you or maybe smack up against you
who was listening and maybe half believing
some of them? Well, you (*who think you can't sing*
or play or dance or remember the right words),
go ask poets to tell you what you're doing
is acting out what they call making a poem.

Being a Model

An old friend said if I didn't have anything
better to do, I should see the photographer.
I didn't have anything, and he was sitting

in an old schoolroom. He said he was taking shots
for magazine adverts all over the world,
had already shot a hundred or more actors

that very morning, and rolled his eyes.
He looked me over, with and without our glasses,
and said I could be somebody. I could run

a bookstore maybe. He wanted to shoot me leaning
forward and looking straight into his lens
and click click click again through an atmosphere

chalky with lessons passed and failed for years
and click click click I could be a kind of professor
or somebody trying to think hard about something.

He made quick notes. He said I'd be on file.
He'd be in touch. It might be all of a week
or maybe never. I said I'd keep him in mind.

On the Persistence of Metaphor

Is everything we think
we know as certain truth
    a metaphor we make
    between our capable hands
and our heads? We recognize
resemblances, and whatever
    we do or see is like
    something we did or saw
before, and isn't it strange
to realize we're repeating
    ourselves, working and dreaming
    in tandem, in ways
we're trying to give names to
as we bring our cupped palms
    full of cold water
    up against our faces
and feel the chilling
relief of lifelessness
    and shut our eyes
    and try to blink it away
as if we might be happy
to have a clearer look
    again at what's going on
    around us in broad daylight?

Long Overdue Praise for Her

She knew where it was,
that thing you were looking for,
and if it wasn't there
   she could tell you just how long
   you'd have to wait for it
   to be yours, not quite
long enough to finish perhaps
or as long as you could hope for,
but in either case
   you would hear from her
   when she wanted it back
   as soon as (or even sooner)
than possible. If you became
over time familiar
with her ways and obeyed
   the rules and even understood
   why they were hers, who knew
   when time was up,
who could keep quiet
or at least hold his speaking voice
down, who could go without
   food or drink, who could show
   the proper attitudes
   of polite attention
or even of being lost
in thought, she would give you
for a while whatever
   you might desire within
   reason, and if it turned out
   to be what you really hadn't

been looking for at all,
she would take it back
without the least sign
      of resentment (perhaps a sigh),
      within the natural bounds
      of the love of propriety,
she would give you almost anything
else you might still have
in mind, this good librarian.

Orpheus Practicing

After he'd strung the turtle shell with catgut,
the ends of his numb fingers (which he'd thought
he knew how to bring together and tell apart)
had trouble deciding which of the strings to pluck
and which to press down on. But because
he'd been swearing with it, his ordinarily
so-so baritone voice had soured, had gone
to hell and back and kept refusing to meet
or match the strains he could still hear in his head.

He sat down on a rock and tried his damnedest
to think about something else. He thought of the woods.
He thought of weather. He thought of picking daisies.
He thought of selling his lute and leaving home
and going to sea and forgetting about all this
music business, all this mechanical strumming
sharp and flat and this memorizing
and rearranging the picking at dull tunes.

Meanwhile, behind his back, the trees bowed down.
Snow melted on the mountains. Wildflowers flourished
in a constant springtime, and the noisy ocean
lowered the crests of its waves and paused to listen.

Listening

You begin not hearing things,
            which is bad enough, but then you begin
                  hearing things, and it suddenly seems
things don't want to be heard
            but become more quiet
                  even while you're listening
as hard as you can
            to the unaccountably soft sounds
                  of what didn't used to be
soft at all, but sharp or flat
            or sharp edged or flat-out plain
                  offensive and too loud. These announcements
have been moderated and are flowing through
            an aging process — no muttering
                  insincerely apologetic disclaimers
of any need for attention — are being wrapped
            and rewrapped in mufflers
                  and taken outdoors for a breath of air,
which, especially in winter, may be vibrant
            with the white noise and the equally beautifully
                  white silence of snow.

Signing

Do they catch their hands
muttering sometimes
when they're not signing, their fingers
     whispering to each other
     or trying to tell whoever
     that might be at the other end
of an arm what they've forgotten
and must remember? Do they
hesitate to go on saying
     what they won't have the slightest
     chance of meaning tomorrow?
     Do slips of the fingers count
against them? Do they practice
sleights of hand? Do they slur
under the influence
     of second thoughts or do battle
     almost helplessly
     with those quicker to reach
conclusions, with interrupters,
with careless, heavy thinkers,
with ambiguous partners
     or strangers? It must be easy
     to babble or go crazy
     without half trying, but how
can lovers hold hands
unless they mean to go
quietly all the way?

Never Let Your Characters Sit Down

Guy Bolton's advice to comedy playwrights

Once they do, they start thinking
of what they thought they thought
were ideas but happen to be
      something less. They start feeling
      wronged and begin explaining
      to whoever that might be sitting
on the other furniture
how they'd been right all along
about being wronged and how
      it wouldn't be long now
      before they turned out to have been
      more than right, and the playwright
would be certain the audience
would hang on every word
about these serious hang-ups
      and misconstruings and mullings
      over immobile regrets
      when even the ticket takers
and ushers could have told him
before the first rehearsal
what they really longed for
      was to see some people acting,
      not like themselves, but stalking
      off and reappearing
suddenly in other doorways
or clambering through windows
or running upstairs, not mincing

words, but on limber toes
　　　or, if they flopped, getting up
　　　again, dead or alive, and asking
and firmly expecting a lover
to lie down too, to keep moving
and moving before it's curtains.

At the Farewell Performance of Henry Ellsworth Robinson, the Magician Known as Ching Ling Soo

The famous man who caught bullets in his teeth
    said through his interpreter there was nothing
      to it, not for one who had the gift,
because didn't jugglers have amazing eyes
    and keep track of the thinner ends of their
      dumbbells
        whirling in all directions? Well, he could see
bullets coming, and he knew just when
    to open his incisors at the exact
      instant to catch the blunt end
of a whirling projectile speeding at him
    from one side of a stage
      to the other. How many matinees
and opening and closing nights did he have
    to prove it before skeptics stopped whispering,
      It's all a trick. He isn't in any danger.
This is for showing off and to sell tickets.
    The man with the rifle isn't really a colonel.
      Consider the laws of physics.
If a bullet traveling x yards per second,
    rotating on its longitudinal axis,
      weighing at impact something like x tons
hit anyone in the teeth, his flashy smile
    would have a hole in it all the way through
      the back of his neck, and somewhere off in the wings
somebody'd have to duck. This is for money.
    Easy marks love to bite their fingernails
      and scream. Some suckers love to believe
Death wants to be a master of ceremonies

for a vaudeville act. Sit down. Calm down.
That isn't real blood.
Those are assistants bending over him,
and those are stagehands putting him on a stretcher.
In a minute he'll come out and cackle at you.

Before the Poetry Reading

They've left me standing in the hall, alone,
outside the room where I'm going to put myself
and some poems on display. The man in charge
is making sure the microphone is too short
and the table holding the lectern has one leg
just short enough.
                          I shouldn't be nervous now
(though I used to watch my teacher, Theodore Roethke,
throw up before readings), and why did I remember
Stanley Kunitz telling me he'd searched
through almost a whole Animal Husbandry building,
up and around and down stairs and more stairs
before a reading, hunting a men's room
so he wouldn't disgrace American poetry
onstage in public? He finally found a door
in a dark basement labeled SWINE.
                                           I'm trying
to think of almost anything other than
what's about to happen. Tonight's hallway
belongs to Natural History. Behind my back
they've stuffed a display case full of local birds
on glass shelves, all of them glassy-eyed,
staring at me and past me at late arrivals
who are mostly polite enough not to stare back
at birds like us, though some give a quick glance,
embarrassed, as if they were going to flunk
Advanced Ornithology.
                                A golden plover,
a marsh hawk, a blue jay, a saw-whet owl, and a raven

beside me are posed and poised to defend themselves
against all those inside their critical distance.
From an unlabeled doorway, my keeper beckons.

Striking the Set

After the last night, after the curtain
on the last performance and the last bows
and flowers and recollections of friends
and strangers and critics, the scene changes
under the hands of stagehands who've been waiting
for all these people to get out of the way.

The furniture and all the portable props
have done their duty under the backsides
and in the hands of actors in summer stock
and are going back where they came from, the mirrors
daubed to cut irrelevant reflections,
the practical doors, the unhingeable flats
unscrewed and unbraced, no longer making up
the difference between open and shut eyes
and minds behind them, no longer making a difference
between backstage and on, out front and the lobby,
the stage door, the alley, and the empty street.

Aristotle Comes to a Conclusion

He'd come around again to the idea
      of the Infinite. It annoyed him.
The arguments in its favor
      seemed as inconclusive
as Infinity itself
      and arrived nowhere. Presuming
a reasonable god and arguing
      back and forth, neither man
nor god would start to do
      anything worth doing
without expecting to reach some
      semblance of an end. Therefore,
the universe could not be endless
      or the music of the spheres
would grow too tiresome
      to be beautiful and the Infinite
too tedious for an alert good god
      to keep in mind. Yet the persistence
of circles, the strangely roundabout
      dances of sun and moon
and the eccentric zodiac
      suggested the before-which-nothing
beginnings and the after-which-
      nothing-else ends were meeting
not just themselves but were surrounding
      actors who might be performing
in the theatrically hectic middle
      of an all-but-absurd art form.

3

Going Back to the Sea

It will seem strange at first
going back under water,
    but soon your difficult breathing
    will feel like a birthright,
and you'll settle down
to a more buoyant life
    where each step and each touch
    will be an easy impulse
to give in to. Your body
will discover old proportions,
    old whispered asides,
    sotto voce wheedlings
and *basso profundo* groans,
and even your angriest shouts
    will be dissolved in the wailing,
    the whistling and humming
of others who came back
to their senses. In place of speech
    you'll have your exclusive silence.
    Now the dissolution of shadows
and the scattering of the sun
into ribbons and broken crescents
    will show what swims around you —
    diatoms, plankton, the suspense
of colloidal particles —
and will blur your vision
    momentarily
    into the visionary,
and you'll know why you're here,
why you've grown tired

of breath, earth, and sunlight,
　　tired of your heavy torso
slumping. If you go back
to the glare and the wind, if you flounder
　　ashore on the sand and lift
　　your shape on surprising legs
and finally stand once more,
beached, weighted down,
　　your strange nose in the air,
　　you'll find what's left of yourself
sinking slowly, easily,
into half-sleep once more.

Ashes

In folk tales if you wish
for gold and dream of it
and search for it in the jungle
or dig for it in the mountains
or sail to a strange island
     and come back or climb down
     or come stumbling out
     holding your glittering
     treasure in your hands,
     it turns to ashes. You see it
blow away in the wind
and scatter into nothing.
So what do you say then
to those who watched for you
at the edge of the forest,
     who stayed by the campfire,
     who waited and waited
     on the near shore, wondering
     where you'd gone and why?
     Do you say to them (for the only
comfort you can imagine)
that even if the gold hadn't changed
to what it had always been,
you probably wouldn't know
what to do with it now?
     Or do you go on dreaming
     of that idol covered by vines,
     those veins still glittering
     in a cave or, under the bones,
     what's left in a dead man's chest?

By a Pond

Its face, as calm as the air,
holds an inverted world
of trees and a trembling sky,
and I'm looking at a garden
as far away from my eyes
as if I lay underwater.

What the seers and sibyls learned
in their rippling mirrors no one
can say for sure. A dropped stone
would send it flying and show
where the earth begins again.

All I can ask for answers
from what I see in my mirror
are the shades of apple blossoms
over which water striders
lighten the touch of bees
against the mud of heaven.

By a Creek

But I'm not there. Right now
I'm sitting in a room
alone, remembering
being there. I can feel
absolutely sure that creek
is rushing forward, pausing
in hollows, turning over
and under itself and pouring
whatever it has to give
in whatever order water
manages to perform whatever
whitens into a constant
cascade of what it was
all along and is and is
going to be again
and again. It comforted
and bewildered me, both
of me, at the same time,
year after year. It kept saying,
I'm here. I wasn't here
an instant ago, but now
I'm here and gone. I'm going
to be here again this moment,
and already I'm falling
out of the same place
I'm going to be always.

The Cherry Tree

Out of the nursery and into the garden
where it rooted and survived its first hard winter,
then a few years of freedom while it blossomed,
put out its first tentative branches, withstood
the insects and the poisons for insects,
developed strange ideas about its height
and suffered the pruning of its quirks and clutters,
its self-indulgent thrusts
and the infighting of stems at cross-purposes
year after year. Each April it forgot
why it couldn't do what it was meant to do,
and always after blossoms, fruit, and leaf-fall
had to be shown once more where not to grow.

Its oldest branches now, the ones carved only
by the rain and wind, are sending stubborn shoots
straight up, blood red, into the light again.

In a Greenhouse

Nurserymen tell us trees
grown under glass
in the calm of a greenhouse
     are spindlier, their trunks
     more modest, more inclined
     to bend under the burdens
of new branches and leaves,
their ordinarily haphazard
outgrowth unbalanced
     in the direction of sunlight
     exclusively, taking no part
     in the play of weather
outside the windows. Inside,
trees that have grown accustomed
to constant temperature
     and easygoing air
     become much less sturdy
     than wild ones subjected
to sudden changes, surprises
of much too much, too little
or too late. Yet their caretakers
     behind glass have discovered
     if they hold the privileged ones
     in hand and shake them,
shake them, even pound them
with padded mallets, they straighten,
stiffen, and grow tall.

Rain Dance in a Rain Forest

We'd have to dance beforehand anywhere else,
      but here, where rain is already happening,
         how simple it all seems to persuade the gods
to bring their heaven down, to shower us
      with that most comfortable answer to a prayer:
         results before the fact. These gods don't need
loud noises and sudden flashes and backlashes
      or bumptious, hogbacking, wind-shearing violence
         in their upper reaches, no vividly lustrous
showing off or any clodhopping, trough-keeping
      worshippers under them. In our boots and raincoats
         we can enjoy being light on our tangled feet
anywhere in routines we don't have to learn,
      movements with no mistakes or traditional steps,
         where the postures of our interdependent torsos
are left to our desires and imaginations,
      and we can be at the heart of a constant stream,
         between its source and its mouth, dancing forever.

Dust Devil

Through stubble the color of dust, the dust devil
spins down the sloping furrows, the only cloud
at this day's end gone furious under the sky
and on earth in a coil toward me, snarled
tight at the churning base, one streamer
flung up and around and lost and left
with a hunch and hump sideslipping
to tanglefoot past me full of itself
and tall as a house with nothing
and no one home long enough
to matter in its hurry to be
done with it, to outrace
what it lifts, swivels,
and tosses to earth
to settle for less
and less, now
for even
less.

Your Tree

When you've chosen it, the one
you want to chop down
and trim to its essentials
and haul away and slice
      to pieces, the forest will wait
      around you, well aware
      of what you're doing. It knows
      competition, light and shade,
and won't interfere
as you pause there
where the roots go underground,
where the solid trunk begins,
      to calculate where your chain saw
      should make its way through bark,
      phloem, cambium, xylem,
      and into heartwood. Your tree
will hold still
while you make the undercut
and may even take for granted
you have some kind of reason
      for what you've chosen to do,
      but if you decide too far
      ahead of time which way
      you're going to start running
when your tree gives in
to gravity, when it begins
losing its firm hold
on the balance of nature,

when it shudders and hesitates
and tilts and twists oddly,
it may surprise you
with an unpredictable swivel
being determined by
asymmetrical branches
in a direction you couldn't foresee
or foretell, no matter how long
or hard you tried, and bring you
down to earth along
with it as just another
renewable resource.

Meeting a Stranger

You find a path. You follow it.
It turns as faint as you are.
You see this stranger
walking toward you
from nowhere and frowning
as if you shouldn't be there
but should get out of the way.
You realize you've been talking
to yourself, even singing.
You've broken his silence
by breaking yours.
You lower your eyes.
You turn your face aside.
You smile. You offer him
your no-longer-bleeding,
more or less clean hand.
He shakes his head.
He keeps his distance.
He edges around you.
You try to tell him
you're lost. Nothing but breath
comes out of your mouth and his.

Panic

Something
is watching you. Something
is ready to savage you. You can't see
any difference in choosing one direction
instead of another, but it's in your nature to climb
out of reach or confuse the enemy by taking cover,
by trying to blend in, by taking on the colors and shapes
of what seems to get along with the here and now or to turn
bright and beautiful, to be deserving of protection and preservation
or suddenly to seem unwholesome, inedible, dangerous, poisonous,
and you don't have time to stand still. The impulse is to run fast enough
and far enough to get out of the woods where you haven't been on speaking terms
with the inaudible and the nameless, and so you follow yourself and find yourself
following an urge toward a sunset, toward the ominous reddening of the leaves
overhead, meaning an inevitable darkness in league with the same darkness
now overtaking you and bringing you to a halt where you crouch
and settle for anything less than our own dimensions,
for the smallest unit of available space
where you plant your feet,
then plant your knees,
where you can bury
your poor head
in your hands.

Among Brambles

Thorns are modified leaves.

HELENA CURTIS AND N. SUE BARNES, *INVITATION TO BIOLOGY*

They gave up opening and spreading themselves
    and being hungry for sunlight long ago
    and went shrinking back
to their branches, hooking and hardening,
    and from then on, eaters of green leaves
    and travelers have paid the price
of snags or of having their tongues bitten
    by other teeth. So I'm stuck this morning
    among brambles, a victim
of my own lack of attention, my irrelevant
    curiosity in the woods. My choices now
    are to go back backward
without turning around (theoretically
    that should unhook me but probably won't)
    or to stride more forcefully and determinedly
forward, overmatching their stubbornness,
    or I can try sideways
    in the surely uncertain hope of the disengagement
of all forces, a simple exchange of opinions
    between those standing still and a creature like me
    who wants to take some kind of personal space
through other equally firmly held ideas
    of personal space and out of it past whatever
    that was to wherever it was I thought I was going.

Foxhole

If you're digging yours in a hurry
        under fire or the expectation
of fire, you make as much of it
        as possible, for obvious reasons,
lying prone. The pointed end
        of your trenching tool and its handle
were designed to replace
        the leverage of your hips
and knees with your far handier
        braces of wrists and elbows
and the heave of shoulders. You don't need
        to be told how big around
or how deep the hole should be
        or which end of your body
goes in first or whether your head
        and helmet should be below
ground level. And once you're inside
        you'll have time, as morning
and afternoon turn into evening
        and night, as the crack and rattle,
crumping and booming go on
        and on, to think of the namesake
of this tactical device. He
        would have dug it somewhere else,
at a scene of his own choosing,
        well in advance of enemies,
and in an emergency
        it would have needed no more
digging at all to furnish
        a place to outwait daylight

and outwit night. He would have made his
    of natural labyrinths in rock slides
and would have what you don't now:
    more than one exit.

Photographing Snakes

They'll seem to pose for you,
though they're always posed
in their own ulterior ways,
in a steadily calm abstraction
of available light. They belong
to what they're lying on,
looking like nothing
on earth among other things,
and they arrange themselves
with what has been rearranged
repeatedly by the wind
and the time-stopped intervals
among seasons. How they appear
when they reappear on paper
means nothing to them. They look
always their best or their least
and don't want to be thought of
at all ahead of time
or remembered after
or recognized at once
as being more powerful,
dangerous, or desirable
than they already are
in the shade or the half shade
out from under the sun
where they've learned to pay
the closest kind of attention
to lying still, regardless
of sudden flashes of light.

What the Marine Biologist Told Me

Those earliest, supposedly daring, ingenious
prehuman ancestors of ours, whom we've pictured
bellying in a lizardly way ashore,

growing new kinds of gills on newfound land,
were really all trying desperately to crawl
back underwater. They didn't want to be stranded

out in the open where there was nothing to eat
but mud and sand, where the very idea of breathing
something so light and empty was beyond them.

But the ocean's edge was pulling out from under.
It slid farther and farther away. What managed
to stay behind was bigger and hungrier

than they were, so they finally had to spend
all day, all night, drinking in this new weather,
learning to wriggle and dig and hunt for each other.

Thoreau and the Mud Turtle

The muddy nest was empty except for one
      inch and a half–long hatchling at the edge,
         motionless. He knelt beside it,
wondering what was wrong. There was no trace
      of the others. They'd either made the dry,
         dangerous, long journey
to the brook or they'd been caught by crows
      or otters. He lifted this runt of the litter
         from among the empty eggshells and watched it crawl
one slow foot per minute. Whenever he moved
      even an inch, it froze,
         pulled in its beak and legs, and waited.
He waited too, till its green head came out
      and looked, listened, then wrong-headedly
         chose a longer way to the brook. He scolded it,
picked it up, and went marching to the shore,
      but hesitated there, afraid
         he might be thwarting nature's merciless plan
that had left the weakest to die
      for the sake of stronger, smarter,
         and quicker turtles to come. So he set it down
and let it choose. It held still for a moment,
      then suddenly turned and scuttled into the current,
         tilted, swirled, and was spun away downstream.

Thoreau and the Loose Cow

He watched her break a fence and leave her pasture.
He watched her cross a bridge and a muddy meadow
ahead of a farmer yelling and switching at her.
He heard himself urging her to go on
escaping, to vanish and stay escaped somewhere
and not come back to her farm and the cow path
and the cow shed and the rusty, empty milk pail,
to lead a larger life.
                 He admired all cows.
They'd been like calm companions when he'd trespassed
the fields they browsed. They were as interested
in grass and weeds as he was. They didn't need
to be entertained, paid little attention to him
and demanded none.
                    But this loose cow had something
more important in mind. She ignored switches
and barking dogs. And she was swimming now —
he couldn't believe it — two hundred yards of river,
holding her nose and horns above the water,
then wading, waddling, stumbling ashore and breaking
another fence. He hoped she might be going
back to the woods like one of her ancestors.

But he turned away, disappointed, when she stopped
among other cows and lowered her head in clover.

Thoreau and the Lightning

The white ash tree, the one he'd visited
    time after time and season after season
and had studied and admired like a proud father,
    had been struck by lightning. Lightning
had gouged downward, tossing broken limbs
    every which way, had split the trunk
into six twenty-foot, splayed, upstanding fence rails
    still held up by the roots, had ploughed a furrow
into a cellar (where it scorched the milk pans),
    had bolted out in a shower of soil, had shattered
weatherboards and beams and the foundation,
    had smashed a shed, unstacked and scattered a woodpile,
had flung pieces of bark two hundred feet
    in all directions. It had thrown into disorder
or destroyed in a moment what an honest farmer
    had struggled for years to gather, and had killed
a great tree. Was he supposed to be humbled
    by the benign, malign, inscrutable purposes
of the Source, the blundering Maker of Thunderheads,
    and be glad he hadn't been standing under it?

The Fly

I'm reading in bed, expecting the usual sequence
    of alert understanding, slight loss of support
        from my mind's eye, and then the gradually
deepening misunderstanding
    of what these words might mean,
        when a fly buzzes
between me and the lamp and wakens me
    with his angry-sounding, insane, desperate
        sound effects. The rest of the house
is dark. He must have come
    to the only beckoning available light
        to do whatever that is he's thinking
he has to do by himself
    before morning. He flies left
        and right and around
from wall to ceiling and circles the brim
    of the shade, unable to bear for long
        the source of his extravagant longing,
and out of fear of the loss of a whole night's sleep
    and while I'm still hearing, in spite of myself,
        his hysterical declaration of what may be
love or at least a passionate desire,
    I switch off the light. Before I can even
        lower the back of my old brain to the pillow,
the sound of his wings stops
    cold. I imagine him
        startled in midflight, instantly
cut off from frenzy, from the whole idea
    of going anywhere. As I settle
        into the hope of losing myself, I wonder

what he's doing now. Has he decided
        in this nearly complete darkness to freeze
            in midair, not to collide
headfirst with some invisible Sheetrock,
        to nose-dive as gently as he can, to flutter
            down into the utterly unknown like me?

At the Ostrich Farm

They're gliding slowly our way
inside the chicken wire,
eleven of them, their necks
eight feet tall. They fluff
their small wings and flirt them
as if almost remembering
how to fly. Their knobby knees
dip backward. They thrust ahead
their one and a half big toes
and stop beside us. Twenty-two
long-lashed bulging eyes
are gleaming and waiting
for the smallest, slightest symptom
of food. My daughters are standing
still for the first time
in living recollection,
their sneakers fixed, asking
no questions, telling no lies,
both staring like ostriches.

No creature on either side
of the wire can quite believe
in the others. Now all at once
all twenty-six eyes are looking
at me, astonished, demanding
some explanation. Behind us
a truck driver stands on his brakes
and honks his horn, and all those ostrich legs
are bending, bracing, and whirling off before the fusses
and feathers attached to them have ballooned and wheeled

and followed their partners through the dust at a gallop as fast
as horses away to the end of their corral and clustered together
beside the shack and the chicken house and the trailer
where someone utterly detached lies dreaming
of ostrich burgers for sale some afternoon.

Pig Dance

This pig would rather not
even think about it,
would rather just stand still
      foursquare or flop down
      gradually on one side
      or the other and let whatever
wants to happen
happen to an old sow
who has seen far better days
      go by, some slowly
      and some much, much
      more slowly, who has never really
supposed her hind trotters
could put her up to this,
though she was born believing
      in the power of firm hams
      and the even more surprising
      resilience and unforeseeable
twistiness of her tail
whose subtly tufted end
knows all about misdirection,
      and just look — her snout can be pointed
      up at the clear sky
      and be held there, kept held there
while all the rest of her
inimitable figure rises
to the vertical and sways
      and swivels just long enough
      to wriggle around and prove
      she can do whatever she wants to

for a sweet while, at least,
can trot around and about
and make music out of mud.

The Last Good Hour of a Worker Bee

If you sit still beside water,
no matter whether
you're in the deep woods
      or your own shallow garden,
      something strange, something
      you couldn't quite have
imagined, will happen.
You may be waiting
and waiting for no reason
but to keep some time
      to yourself as it slips by,
      and a bee, a black-and-gold
worker who has been finding
and gathering its share
of a flowering morning
      (as it had yesterday
      and as only it knows how),
      may fall down past your shoulder
onto the same light surface
your eyes have had in mind
for nearly a solid hour
      or forever (you won't be sure),
      and it may struggle there
      with its uncanny wings,
apparently almost
as surprised as you are
at where it's found itself
      afloat on the upper edge
      of an underworld where bees
      have little to do with nectar

except for small reflections,
and maybe the water striders,
those long-legged flies that fly
  between water and air,
  will show you, leg by wing,
  half-thorax by mandible,
minute by minute, eye
after eye after eye, how we share
with each other what we are.

The Dead

Always finding them on the shore. The grebes and scoters.
The salmon at ease at last on their cold sides.

They won't go away. The owls and skinned beavers
in the woods. The quail no longer scurrying.

The hawks hung upside down on the barbed wire.
The frogs and toads all gone to an old silence.

Raccoons and possums by the side of the road.
The weasel in the driveway. The rabbit's ear.

The burro flat in the orchard. The lost dogs.
They won't stop dying. They go on and on

dying and waiting for me to do something
instead of just saying they'd begin again,

be beautiful again, that empty promise,
that momentarily tasteful mouthful

of dust I've fed on all these years. They're still
dead back there and are still becoming

dead as long as I last and will keep on dying
till there isn't anything left to remember with.

4

This Is Only a Test

Whatever frightened you, whatever you thought
might happen someday, is not happening now.

This is only a test so we can be sure
we can tell you when we think it's happening

before it does or at least no later than
simultaneously. What you should do

(when you hear the official sound we're about to make
at almost any moment) is to listen

as closely as you can, then tell yourself
This is what it's going to sound like

when it might happen. You'll remember how
to hear yourself thinking if it ever does.

Marksmanship

The silhouette of a crouching man
        rising out of the ground, facing you,
            had better be recognizable
immediately as an enemy
        darker than you, aiming something
            lethal your way, and in the split second
crucial to any good student of marksmanship,
        you have to be already killing
            this simulacrum of a human being
before *it* can kill *you*. If you're lucky
        and good enough, it will go keeling backward
            and flatten itself like the dead. But be prepared
for it to rise instantly, immortal, to face you,
        ready to fire whatever that might be
            it's clutching in its hands, so you have to keep
killing it and killing it again, and even again
        as it falls back and comes flapping up once more
            and you have to fire till your small arms are empty.

Under Fire

Because you heard the shot,
you know it missed you, and so
      you have to decide now
      (not later on)
whether to fall down
or duck and run,
      so if you're near cover,
      go for it flat out
and stay there till you know
who, where, and how far,
      but if you're out in the open
      and haven't been hit, fall
anyway. Lie still. No,
lie still. And don't look.
      You're going to have to think
      about how to be dead.
Someone's watching you,
your head or your heart on a cross
      or the base of a steel notch,
      deciding what to do next,
which will depend on you,
on whether you move your hand
      or foot or open your eyes,
      on what you make of yourself
and how long it's going to take
and what you have in mind.

At Dawn on the Fifth of July

At the dead end of the street
charred cones and cylinders,
no longer explosive fragments
of spheres and nuggets, the pavement
covered with colored scars
from flashes and booms and whistles,
from all the Crackling Sams,
from Hopalong Knuckle Dusters,
from Grunts—an after-the-crazy,
the-hell-with-it banquet look—
and the independent birds
all gone now into hiding
till the end of the world is over.

Fighting the Blizzard

Police jargon for being drunk

A homeless drinking man
    trying to go somewhere
like home at night will take
    his first step
in one or two of the four
    official directions
and his second
    toward almost anywhere
but the first and the third
    and eventually will establish
a kind of balance
    among opposing forces
while he starts looking for work
    in a vestibule or doorway
or Dumpster or unlocked car
    or wherever enough dead leaves
can be heaped into a bed
    without breakfast, so there he is
engaged in reexploring
    the unknown, still knowing not
to fight with an old blizzard
    but to take the enduring way,
which is stopping, making a house
    out of the blizzard itself
or a cave into a snowdrift
    to sleep in before he's lost.

Rooming with Jesus

Though he would have no clothes worth borrowing
except for amusement, he wouldn't borrow yours
and leave them scattered around, unwashed.
He would forgive you for making impolite noises
and listen to any exaggerated entries
in your overlong, untitled, unpublished,
and unpublishable autobiography
with its anecdotes about schools and carnal love
with a straight, polite face. When the rent was due
and you needed to render unto the landlord
what was the landlord's, he would forgive and forget
if you forgot or didn't or couldn't give,
and he would clean up after himself. If you didn't,
he would do it for you, and you'd feel guilty,
naturally, and most certainly move out
when he gave shelter to beggars, thieves, crackpots,
lepers, down-and-out whores, or you again.

Running the Four Hundred Meters

You had to use breath
you didn't have
enough of meanwhile
staying in one lane
of cinders running
so far ahead of you
you couldn't believe
you were supposed to
catch up to where
it seemed to be going
without you without
the loss of your lungs
your feet no longer
yours your whole body
longing for a tape
suspended across a line
you could see but had no sense
you could ever touch
without dying and being
transformed into a creature
of a higher lower order
with wings or more legs
than these two shreds
at the ends of you and yours
which had almost disappeared.

Life Class

The more we look at her, the more we wonder
whether her arms are hers, whether her shoulders
and the smooth lines of her back are really hers
or ours on pages where we smudge her likeness
hour after hour. We study all of her
as if we knew our eyes were deceiving us.

They are. The more we look, the more we know
we've never known what she is. Her downcast eyes
are saying she's under assault by all these strangers
gathering every shade and reappearance
of light along her body. She's being revised
to a few principal parts, mismanaged, stiffened,
oversimplified and made little of,
distorted, rendered helpless, reconsidered,
erased, even torn in half. She's holding still,

but she's being paid to hold still, the best defense
some creatures have against death: to disappear,
to become whatever surrounds them. When they move,
they're lost. And now we lose her. She finds herself
out from under our eyes, dressing in shadows.

Overheard at Dinner in the Home of a Recent Widow

> Since it is almost impossible to seat twelve in the house of
> a widow who appoints a member of her family or a very
> intimate friend to take the place of host to avoid serving
> herself from an untouched first dish, it is now considered
> essential to consider the lady of honor the one who is seated
> on the right of the gentleman of honor, who sits on the right
> of the hostess.
>
> EMILY POST, *ETIQUETTE*

My dear, I know I'm not supposed to be
    sitting beside you. This place is reserved
        for some preoccupied gentleman of honor,
one of whose hands should be, on the other hand,
    intimately touched by someone or other,
        and since it's nearly impossible to serve
anything or anyone without touching,
    let me say in whichever ear that is
        you've turned toward me, the others in this room
all knew your deceased husband for what he was,
    but no one knows the place of the dead better
        than I do, and you have my hand on it.

The Minutes of the Last Meeting

In the hours of the last meeting, we all wondered
what to do with our hands. Flat on the table?
In our laps? Or with fingers interlaced
yet set to spring into action like clipboards?
We knew where our feet should be: both on the floor.
But our hands remained a problem. They were shifty.
So we used them to put new papers in old order
in order to shift them over and back under
the uppermost for the tips of rollerballs.
We underlined the words that hadn't already
been underlined. We checked. We circled bullets
to make for an even greater emphasis
on the obviously essential elements
of elemental essentials. We discussed them
more than once, then voted. Then we nodded
more than once in the general direction
of our general director, our resourceful
source, the founding father of our foundation,
and generally agreed we were dismissed.

A Preface to the History of Chairs

If all day you'd been kneeling
and crouching behind trees
or bushes or crawling through grass
and suddenly straightening
      your spine and your knees and running
      hard and fast, coming close
      (before you tried to kill it)
      to the wild game also running
hard, harder and faster
than you could, wouldn't you
have been thinking of somewhere
not to stoop or hunker,
      or sit on your heels
      or flop down altogether,
      but to take a load off your feet
      and lower yourself closer
to the earth, bending at least four
of your hinges and maybe resting
the more fully padded ones,
not down on a stone,
      but maybe a dry stump
      you'd found and remembered
      and hollowed beforehand
      or had learned to duplicate
from pieces of itself,
a place you could be at ease
but halfway standing up,
half ready to make tracks?

By the Empty Stone

He walks away with the sword. He's smiling
innocently, and the rest of us are left
to watch him already growing larger than life,
already being fawned over
by an entourage whose elbows bump and gouge
to claim their places in a royal procession.

Some who lost are running to catch up,
to be dogs under his table, scrapping for bones
and droppings, and I'm left all to myself
by the empty stone. There's nothing magical
about the hole where the sword was. I can feel
the ordinary roughness of the basalt.
No lizard or wizard bites me, and nothing at all
explains what kept that sword he's waving now
stuck where it was for years against our wills,
against our twisting and yanking. The obvious answer
is *we* loosened it for him. He was made king
by the luck of the draw, no matter how willingly
he put it back when we cried *Foul!* and no matter
how many times he took it out again
when none of us could. It was good timing
or blind luck. And though some others who lost
are straggling back to their cows and their milkmaids,
to their hearthsides and kitchen stuff, to swilling
their sows like the hogs they are, I'm staying here
all night, if I must, to prove it was a trick.

Pounding Swords into Ploughshares

You'll need dozens for each ploughshare,
but no matter how hard your hammer
    comes down on them, pounding
    and pounding blades on an anvil,
no matter how glowing they look there,
bloodred again, they'll only flatten
    to thinner and thinner, misshapen,
    flabby sheets useless for anything
but the sheer noise of forging them
or patching roofs. Their crystal structure
    may give in at half the temperature
    of melting, but simple annealing
won't bring their shapes together
and sharpen them to a hollow
    earth-turning curve. In the meanwhile,
    the dozens and dozens you took them from,
the ones not dead yet, will be demanding
you give them back, supposedly
    to protect their unploughed farms
    from the enemy, but much more likely
to flourish in someone else's fields
among their abandoned ploughs.

The Salute

Your right arm rises till the humerus
is horizontal, the radius and ulna
      aligned with the metacarpals
      and phalanges, including the thumb,
the elbow crooked slightly forward
and the right forefingertip
      mid-eyebrow till your superior
      has decided to mimic you,
or not, at which time you will give
a snappy forward jerk of the forearm
      and return it to the thigh. If the salute
      occurs in a stationary, fixed
confrontation, your about-face
will be executed smartly. If you are passing
      outdoors, you will continue walking.
      Your mouth will remain shut.
Your lips will stay level. Whatever that may be
going on and on in your mind by then
      will keep going on, but only
      in private. You will not look back.

Instructions for the Caretaker

The corpse on the sofa and the corpse in the bathtub
should be removed and the upholstery
and enamel cleansed, and the older corpse
in the tool shed should be moved to a shallow grave
between the daisies and the begonias,
what's left of one foot exposed among the leaves.
The corpse in the attic may be left as is.

The revolving bookcase and the sliding panels
in the den and the hinged eyes in family portraits
should be lubricated with wax or mineral oil.
The medicines in the bathrooms—all of those labeled
as analgesics, balms, or soporifics—
should be refreshed to minimum lethal doses.

The ectoplasm in the basement tub
should be unfolded and the dumbwaiter
tested with a trial lift to the hatch
by the dining room table, and the table itself
lightened and rewired to the echo chamber.

The associates will arrive by underground
passageways or by open bedroom windows
and will require from you only your silence.
After you've admitted the newlyweds,
who will arrive by coach at the front door,
you may hang yourself as usual in the cloakroom.

On the Road

The road of excess leads to the palace of wisdom.
WILLIAM BLAKE, *THE MARRIAGE OF HEAVEN AND HELL*

There were too many of us in the wagons, and we had all this baggage
everyone swore was essential, and of course we'd had too much to eat
and too much (some thought that was impossible) to drink before and after
we could get started, and all of us had taken the liberty of inviting
camp followers and wingmen, trailers and flankers, who'd given their all
at the office, who'd overfilled their quotas and bettered all the demands
of bonus contracts, who'd so far exceeded their grasps, they couldn't hold
tight to the best parts of themselves, so when we arrived in a heap
at the raised drawbridge, we covered the whole road and the ditches
on both sides and as far behind us as anyone had the eyes or guts to look,
and we'd filled the moat as high as the first drains of the palace
that should have had a prince and a princess and a king and a queen
waiting for us inside it, showing us how to be wise, but didn't.

A Zodiac for the Twenty-Second Century

We will endure under new signs and wonders.
For Aries, Sheep. For Taurus, Horny Ox.
For Gemini, Septuplets. For Cancer, More Cancer.
For Virgo, Call Girl. Sagittarius, Sniper.
Libra, Short Weight. Scorpio, Radiation.
Pisces, Dead Cod. Aquarius, Dry Well.
Leo, Jackal. Capricorn, Judas Goat.

The Bitter End

It's the part of the rope that goes up and around
and through and then comes back
to the first place (or all those in or out
of sequence) and becomes a knot
      that will hold itself and even something else
      long enough and well enough
      to keep it safe, to keep it from getting away
      (when it might be too heavy)
from doing what it couldn't help feeling
like doing to itself or others, the attachments
and restraints, the grim finales, the choke holds
and hog-ties, yet it's still blamed
      for taking the wrong turns into snarls and slips
      and grannies. The bitter end has learned how
      to get along with having a bad name,
      with being what nobody wants,
what we're afraid might happen
on journeys toward this and that, all those
limp, limping miles to the only place
we can meet the other kind.

5

Lost in Thought on an Extension Ladder

It isn't a good place to forget why
you wanted to climb this high in the first place,
making yourself scarce on solid ground.
Was it new lights or clearing what isn't going
down a downspout into the water cycle?

You can feel (as firm as any step on a stair)
the rungs under your arches. You're not afraid
they're suddenly going to break or disappear
and leave you to the mercy of your grip
on the side rails, sending you back where you came from.
You believe the ladder can hold its own. You believe
each rung knows where it is, that none of them
is a point of no return, that each is at least
as immediately dependable as the last.

But you're backing down now with no loss of stature
in your own shaky opinion. You're playing it safe.
You never wanted to be one of Jacob's angels.
You'll settle for less by going back to the garden.

Off Balance

Something in your head is telling you
you're out from under
      the place where what's left in there
      thought it was
and thought it was going, somewhere
you hadn't planned on
      exactly, and at that moment
      you realize you must change
the whole idea of direction
if you want to be anywhere
      sooner, not later, and must turn
      and not swivel too far
toward this surprising goal
      you hadn't had in mind
      and hadn't considered choosing,
and must keep at least one foot
from losing a track or a trace
      of where the other is
      without thinking about it
in advance. Then, in the steadily
unsteady abrupt resumption
      of more or less forward progress,
      all that's required of you
besides your single-minded
version of locomotion
      is a serene look,
      not at your toes or heels
(though one of them may feel
as light as if it had wings

and the other seems abstract),
but at what lies ahead
where the way is paved for you
with something like good intentions,
something stony, floorlike,
earthy or concrete,
and now undeniably,
unavoidably underfoot.

The First Law of Thermodynamics

When energy is destroyed in one form, it reappears in a corresponding quantity in another.

You can pound it, pound it
down till you think, *Thank god,*
    it's finally gone away,
    or you can shoot it
up in the air and hope
it will keep on going
    and going somewhere else
    and leave you alone
at last, but here it comes
in disguise, not only claiming
    to be your long-lost brother,
    but your father and the father
of your father's children. No matter
how many times you snap
    your wrist and your fingers
    to get rid of the shred
of plastic, it clings there
like flypaper as you grow
    warmer with exercise,
    or you can huff and puff
at a candle flame: the seizure
of the diaphragm is transformed
    into a moving column
    of air, which narrows
between your lips
to send a burning gold

        hydrocarbon crown
        back to the blue beginning
and in its smoky way
into a jangle of molecules,
        leaving you to recover
        your breath in your own darkness.

The General Theory

The two of them are traveling together
in the same direction but in separate trains.
They see each other at night through dusty glass.

One of the trains is going slightly faster.
The inside of each train will seem to each
motionless, but through the glass the other

will obviously be moving farther along.
If either lifts a hand to make a gesture
of recognition, neither will ever know

when it happened or whether it was a product
of the reciprocal relationships
among time, space, and motion. Will its existence

seem as uncertain as what someone might see
from a third place, beside the tracks in the dark,
watching them shrink away to a point of light?

Falling into Place

You're going to bed now
at the quiet end of business
with the default ingredients
of your body, no longer inclined
to follow the example
of molecules or to rub
your sticks and stones together
or bustle about at random.

You'll slowly shrink away
from the obvious to embody
all your philosophy
by turning into a playground
of teeter-totter, swing,
sandbox, and monkey bars,
steep slide and roundabout
play the leading and minor
parts of all the players.

Helping the Home Patient Fall Asleep

Adapted from *Health, Nursing, and Prevention of Disease,*
Blanche Swainhardt, RN, 1926

His stomach should contain
no more than water
or perhaps cooked fruit,
and he should be clad
in a loose, porous garment
so his body may breathe.

You should help him up
gently but firmly
into bed with a coverlet
long enough to tuck in
on a sanitary mattress
under a plumped pillow.

The principle is to warm
his feet and cool his head.
A restful night in bed
is directly proportional
to the absence of blood
from the neck up.

You do not stay nearby
to indulge in conversation
and not, above all else,
to commiserate. You say,
*Forget the public world
and private grievances.*

Think of nothing but pleasure.
Let go of what you're clenching
in your fists. He shouldn't believe
he's holding his bed in the air
with willpower, but should feel
he weighs a thousand pounds.

A Cold Call

Holly is calling me from the cemetery.
She wants to plot my future. She really wants me
to be considerate of my loved ones
in advance, to make all the arrangements
now so none of them will have to feel
the expensive thrill of it at the wrong time,
and she can make a place for me all at once
over the phone and spare every one of us
our pain and awkwardness. The facilities
I wouldn't believe. They're in a sylvan setting,
which means it's like under trees with a very tasteful
horizontal stone so the grass around it
can be mowed off of my name and dates, and a twelve-
(or under)-letter characterization
engraved there (such as *Dearest* or *Beloved*
or in my case *Husband*) would be visibly
permanent regardless of growth. She's offering
today what she won't call a once-in-a-lifetime
discount, but let's face it, it sort of is.

In Memory of His Memory

It was good for the alphabet, state capitals,
and arithmetic. They froze into place somewhere
in a piece of his mind. In speech class and debate
his mind's eye pictured streams of abstract words
that had rattled out of the mouths of orators,
but not by the whole heart. That was for poems.

He could memorize any lyrics, no matter how bad,
with the ease of a quick-study understudy
and later remembered the names under the faces
of students arranged in rows of rows and rows.

He could think, even think and think, and recalibrate
whatever he should have done and hadn't done
in unforgettable moments like this one now.
We've gathered here to pay our last respects
to an absentee whose name you can find somewhere
in your programs. He was called away to do
something I can't recall, and apparently
he did it, or else you and I wouldn't be here.

Coolness under Fire

In memory of Len Roberts

It was the prime virtue
in the world of the young
Hemingways. You didn't
      duck or flinch but kept your head
      when all about you were
      about to lose theirs
without enough time
to say farewell. Instead,
you were to demonstrate
      that you could keep on thinking
      about what really mattered,
      could stand your ground
while managing to be
judicious at the dead center
of what others might be calling
      Danger. You kept your feet
      under you. You used the gift
      of plough-horse sense you were born with
and kept your wits about you,
behind you, beside you, regardless
of the vulgar sounds
      of death coming your way
      and arriving so quickly,
      you had no time to mean less
or more than nothing. Coolness
was also under a fire
in the mountains, along the shore,

or almost anywhere
on bare dirt. You could burn
whatever you liked there
for as long as you liked
and lie down and make love
out of disaster, and still,
under the embers, under the ashes,
the bare earth stayed as cool
as you, then turned cold again.

Our Bodies

Plato believed the gods
    had aimed our eyes and feet
forward because looking
    backward, though necessary
sometimes, was less important
    for the fulfillment of tasks
than getting on with them.
    We were contrived to swivel
suddenly and jump, to hang on
    and wait for the right moment
to let go and run for it.
    Our lateral symmetry
and our bundle of bones
    allowed for that and for simply
walking away, maintaining
    the balance of our burdens
with our well-defined hands
    and fingers, sometimes more
eloquent than our mouths.
    He thought the spherical skull
had been fashioned purposefully
    in the manner of sun and moon
to keep the house of the soul
    from being broken into
by intruders. Our apparatus
    stood to reason and sat
to think better of it, knelt
    to save what little it could,
crouched to be slightly less
    apparent, or lay down

curled to be shut against
          (or at length more open to)
the wisdom of the night.

For Their Second Childhood

There's hardly anybody
      left alive to remind them
        to stop that
slouching to stand up
      straight to quit playing
        with their food to chew it
certain numbers of times
      and swallow
        without gulping
and to know when to go
      to the bathroom and where
        it is and what to wash
and wipe and what to take off
      and put on to be afraid
        their faces will stay like that
or how they ought to start
      thinking seriously
        of the future just in case
they ever get there or what
      for a change to please
        remember for heaven's sake.

In the Nursing Home

After those bad old times,
now, when no one
is telling you what to do
    to earn your keep and before
    even more orderly keepers
    have begun to tell you
(in each ear
and on pieces of paper
delivered by bare hands
    or pinned to the walls
    or inside the only door)
    what today will have to do
with tomorrow—after all
those familiar surprises,
when you find yourself prepared
    at last for opening night
    in darkness at the edge
    of a curtain where stage-light
has brightened a place for you,
where spectators are waiting
through a spirited overture
    and a solemn introduction
    for you to justify
    your appearance and their attention,
you'll show all of them now
or never why they're here
watching and listening.

The Name

When a man or a woman died, something of theirs,
some token—a beaded belt, a pair of moccasins,
a necklace—would be left beside the path
where a hunting party, returning, would see it
and know that name was dead now.

They would remember how to say it,
but not at the campfire, not in stories,
not whispered in the night to anyone else,
but only to themselves.

Then, after years, when the right one had been born,
they would hold that child above the earth
to the four directions and speak the name again.

A Beginner's Guide to Death

You have been taken down
        the first and only step in the learning process,
                so even a raw beginner
like you is already skilled in every aspect
        of our craft. Your envies and temptations
                at last are over. Who wore the best clothes?
Who had all that money? Who knew exactly
        where to go when there was nowhere to go?
                Who could recite all five of the wrong names
of love by heart? Now, even if you tried
        as hard as you once knew how, you won't have time
                to think of any more answers. At one stroke
in the eyes of your only teacher you'll achieve
        a comfortable failure
                and be marked present, absent, and excused forever.

About the Author

David Wagoner has published nineteen previous books of poems, most recently *A Map of the Night* (University of Illinois Press, 2008). He also has published ten novels, one of which, *The Escape Artist,* was made into a movie by Francis Ford Coppola. He won the Ruth Lilly Poetry Prize in 1991, six yearly prizes from *Poetry,* and the Arthur Rense Prize from the American Academy of Arts and Letters in 2011. He was a chancellor of the Academy of American Poets for twenty-three years. He edited *Poetry Northwest* from 1966 to 2002, and he is professor emeritus of English at the University of Washington. He teaches in the low-residency MFA program of the Whidbey Writers Workshop.

 Since 1972, Copper Canyon Press has fostered the work of emerging, established, and world-renowned poets for an expanding audience. The Press thrives with the generous patronage of readers, writers, booksellers, librarians, teachers, students, and funders — everyone who shares the belief that poetry is vital to language and living.

MAJOR SUPPORT HAS BEEN PROVIDED BY:

The Paul G. Allen Family Foundation

Amazon.com

Anonymous

Arcadia Fund

Diana and Jay Broze

Beroz Ferrell & The Point, LLC

Golden Lasso, LLC

Gull Industries, Inc.
on behalf of William and Ruth True

Lannan Foundation

Rhoady and Jeanne Marie Lee

National Endowment for the Arts

New Mexico Community Foundation

Cynthia Lovelace Sears and Frank Buxton

Washington State Arts Commission

Charles and Barbara Wright

To learn more about underwriting Copper Canyon Press titles,
please call 360-385-4925 ext. 103

The Chinese character for poetry is made up of two parts: "word" and "temple." It also serves as pressmark for Copper Canyon Press.

This book is set in Sabon Next, with heads set in Stemple Garamond. Design and composition by Valerie Brewster, Scribe Typography. Printed on archival-quality paper at McNaughton & Gunn, Inc.